D.I.Y. DROPOUTS

D.I.Y. DROPOUTS

Jim Hutchings

A STAR BOOK
published by
the Paperback Division of
W.H. Allen & Co. plc

A Star Book
Published in 1987
by the Paperback Division of
W.H. Allen & Co. plc
44 Hill Street
London W1X 8LB

Copyright © Jim Hutchings, 1987

Printed and bound in Great Britain by
Anchor Brendon Ltd, Tiptree, Essex

ISBN 0 352 32082 6

DEDICATED TO THE HERO
ON THE LAST PAGE WHO
OCCASIONALLY GETS IT
RIGHT.

D.I.Y.?

IT TAKES ALL SORTS....

SOME........

.....CAN AND START BUT NEVER FINISH.

..... CAN'T BUT TRY AND SUCCEED FAIRLY WELL.

AND SOME........

....CAN'T AND DON'T.

AND THE REST...

'Useless? Anytime something needs doing, he writes to Jim'll Fix It!'

'Good God, woman, you're not wanting to redecorate again!'

'Stop moaning, woman. They even built the M25 in *phases*!'

'Well it *was* going to be a serving hatch, but I don't know what he's got in mind now.'

'He has this back trouble, but he says he's OK if he doesn't lift, bend, stoop, stretch or stand too long.'

'This bloke over the road has built his speakers subtly and unobtrusively into the ceiling.'

'You're always the same, cock the job up
and then blame metrification!'

'It was two years ago this month he had this sudden inspiration to make us a through-lounge.'

'I've got the books, Arthur. ARTHUR!'

'Holding the ladder hell! I'm just keeping him at it!'

'Hey, Harry, it's the new neighbour. He wants to borrow some tools!'

'Six weeks ago I half stripped it to motivate
him – but it didn't!'

'Have you tried *allez oop*?'

'Your husband fitted it, you say? Oh dear, oh dear, oh dear. Oh my goodness me!'

'Want to borrow what? A screwdriver?
What sort of screwdriver? Standard, slotted,
crosshead, parallel tip, small stub, a six-inch
starter or an Archimedean spiral ratchet?'

'He hasn't fixed it yet then?'

'And he's useless about the house you say?
Lets things go, won't fix or maintain
anything. Dear oh dear.'

'I'm glad you're coming out next week, Joe, because the sitting room and dining room need decorating and I thought it would be nice to have the ceilings tiled as well. The paintwork in the kitchen has got pretty grubby, so that will need doing, and I've already bought the wallpaper for the hall stairs and the landing...'

'I don't think he intends changing that
washer somehow.'

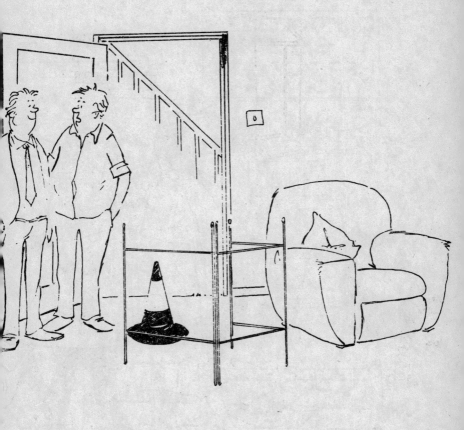

'What a fuss over a loose floorboard, eh?'

'No thanks, dear. There's only one thing that needs replacing in our house!'

'Just the one shelf is it, dear?'

'Do it yourself? Haven't got a lot of bloody choice being born in this age!'

'Look at it this way, duck. If I did all the
jobs you wanted me to do, I'd have nothing
to do at weekends.'

'Cut it wrong again? I expect your ruler's faulty, dear.'

'He says it's broken down – and he's waiting
for the AA.'

'Straighten it up a bit – you're going crooked – more pressure – clear the hole – steady now – check the depth – watch what you're doing!'

'I don't know why he wants a shed – the tools he's got he keeps in a Marks and Spencer's carrier.'

'Mister Fixit's residence.'

'Could I have my hammer-head back, please?'

'Watcha doin' at the weekend, Charlie?'
'Bloody decorating ain't I!'

'OK, OK! I'll put you a sodding shelf up!'

'Mind you, I wouldn't ask her to do
anything I couldn't do myself!'

'I see you've stopped the tap dripping then!'

"'Ere, Daphne, I think you ought to wear
trousers while you're doing the ladder work!'

'Wanna job?'

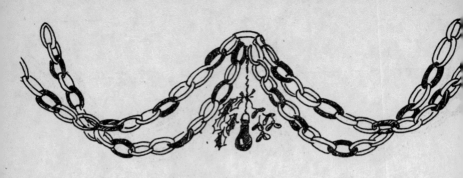

'I told my ol' man you had coloured lights all round your room, so he painted that one.'

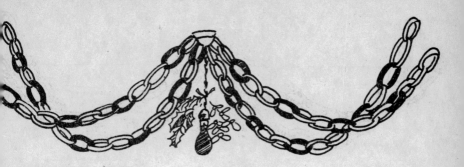

'But our lights flash on and off.'
'I told him that too, so he's going to sit by
the switch.'

'Why don't you try mixing some glue with it, dear?'

'Do it yourself, self-service, pick your own, cash and carry – nobody wants to do anything for you nowadays.'

'And when we get to the D.I.Y. Superstore, head straight for the wallpapers and no funny business.'

'I don't know what the hell you're laughing at – *you've* got to live in it!'

'That old back door sticking again Cynth?'

'Who loves yer, baby?'

'You finally paint the front of the house and everyone has to know about it!'

'Mother's locked herself in the lavatory. Can you deal with that or shall I call the fire brigade?'

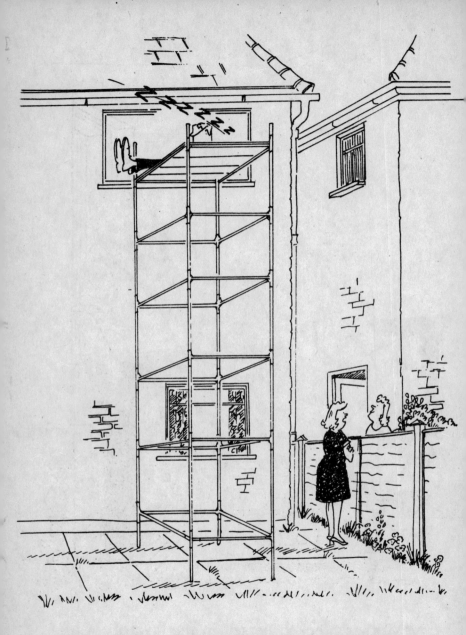

'I don't know why he's hired that – he's got a perfectly good ladder.'

'No, I'd better not. She'll only nag me to put up some shelves.'

'When are you going to fix this damn seat properly? Mother's just fallen off again!'

'Oh no you *won't* skip the bloody wallpapering!'

'As far as he's concerned D.I.Y. stands for
Don't Involve Yourself.'

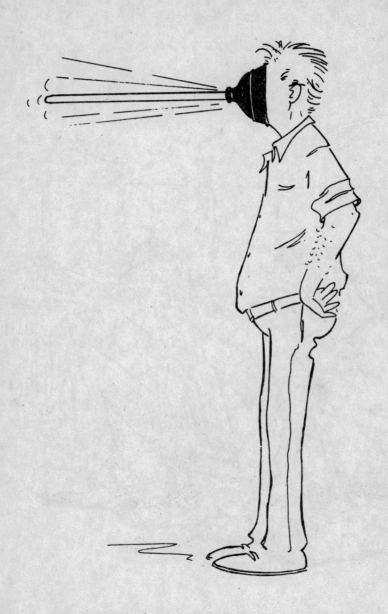

'Just for that you can unblock it yourself!'

'I opted out back in the fifties when yer
D.I.Y. came in.'

'I don't know what you're trying to make,
dear, but the dog doesn't think much of it.'

'You've got a confession to make? Oh God,
I hope it's not that you're useless at D.I.Y!'

'For the last time, are you or are you not
going to put those blasted shelves up?!'

'You didn't tell me your dad was bilingual.'

'I suppose you'll be teaching him to climb the stepladder next.'

'Last year he tried putting in central heating, this year he thought he'd insulate the loft first.'

'With your D.I.Y. record, mate, no chance!'

'I know to err is human, dear, but you err every time you do a job!'

'Get off your father when he's trying to fix the plumbing!'